ISBN-13: 978-1533312457

ISBN-10: 1533312451

17582025R00066

Made in the USA
Middletown, DE
27 November 2018